ESSENTIAL DK COMPUTERS

DIGITAL
MOVIE MAKING

ABOUT THIS BOOK

Digital Movie Making is an easy-to-follow guide to capturing and editing home movies on a PC using Windows Movie Maker, which comes free with Windows Millennium Edition.

EVER DREAMED OF BEING A MOVIE mogul? If you have a digital video camera and a PC with Windows Millennium, you already have all the equipment you need to take the raw video you've recorded on the camera and turn it into a finished, edited home movie, complete with transitions between scenes, titles, narration, and background music. It's easy too. This book explains how to transfer the video from your camera to your computer, how to organize the video into easily edited clips and then how to turn those into a finished movie. It then shows you how you can share your home movie with friends by sending it as an email message or by posting it on a site on the internet.

The chapters and the subsections present the information in the book by using examples, which in almost every instance are accompanied by illustrations that show

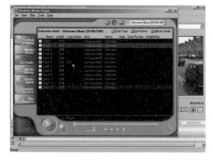

you exactly how the example would appear on-screen.

The book contains several features to help you understand both what is happening and what you need to do.

Command keys, such as ENTER and CTRL, are shown in these rectangles: [Enter ←] and [Ctrl], so that there's no confusion, for example, over whether you should press that key or type the letters "ctrl."

Cross-references are shown in the text as left- or right-hand page icons: ⌐ and ⌐. The page number and the reference are shown at the foot of the page.

As well as the step-by-step sections, there are boxes that explain a feature in detail, and tip boxes that provide alternative ways of doing things. Finally, at the back of the book, you will find a glossary of common terms and a comprehensive index to help you find specific information quickly.

ESSENTIAL DK COMPUTERS

DIGITAL MOVIE MAKING

ROB BEATTIE

LONDON, NEW YORK, MUNICH, MELBOURNE, DELHI

SENIOR EDITOR Jacky Jackson
SENIOR ART EDITOR Sarah Cowley
DTP DESIGNER Julian Dams
PRODUCTION CONTROLLER Michelle Thomas

MANAGING EDITOR Adèle Hayward
SENIOR MANAGING ART EDITOR Karen Self

Produced for Dorling Kindersley Limited by
Design Revolution Limited, Queens Park Villa,
30 West Drive, Brighton, East Sussex BN2 2GE
EDITORIAL DIRECTOR Ian Whitelaw
SENIOR DESIGNER Andrew Easton
PROJECT EDITOR Alison Ali
DESIGNER Paul Bowler

First published in Great Britain in 2002 by
Dorling Kindersley Limited,
80 Strand, London WC2R 0RL

2 4 6 8 10 9 7 5 3 1

A CIP catalogue record for this book is available from the British Library.

ISBN 0-7513-3709-9

Colour reproduced by Colourscan, Singapore
Printed and bound in Italy by Graphicom

For our complete catalogue visit
www.dk.com

CONTENTS

MAKING MOVIES

The popular, but flickery, 8mm home movies are now giving way to more sophisticated movie making that's shot on digital video cameras and edited on home computers.

YOUR HOME MOVIE STUDIO

Home computers are good at crunching numbers and processing words. But they're also excellent at editing almost any kind of digital information – including sound and video. If you want to edit home videos on a computer, you can use an old-style analogue camcorder, but you'll need to buy a special decoder box to sit between the camcorder and the computer to translate the analogue camcorder video into digital signals (the 0s and 1s that the computer understands). The quality will not be as good as a DV camera, but may be adequate for some purposes.

● Now, with the increasing popularity and affordability of digital video cameras, you can get even better results because there's no degradation when you copy the video to the computer. Simply shoot some footage with your DV camera, plug it into your computer, and copy the scenes you've shot across to the hard disk. After that, load up your editing software and you can start to move scenes around, shorten them, add narration, music, titles, and so on.

WHAT KIND OF PC DO I NEED?

A big, fast one. As we'll see, Movie Maker's very clever at compressing video to make it smaller (and thus quicker to transmit as part of an email message, for example) but because it compresses in real time, a reasonably powerful PC with lots of memory is required. Movie Maker's "official" minimum specification is a PC with a 300MHz Pentium II, 64MB of memory, and two gigabytes of free hard disk space. In practice, you should probably double the amount of memory and go for at least a Pentium III-based computer.

● When a movie has finished, you can watch it using whichever movie editing program you used to create it. Or you can save it as a file that can be played back by another program – for example, Windows Media Player (which comes free with Windows ME). Movies can be posted on Zip disks, which are both capacious and affordable, or compressed and sent as attachments to email messages. Alternatively, you can post your movie to a website and invite your friends to "drop by" and view the results.

● Although there are many video-editing programs available, we're going to concentrate on how to use Windows Movie Maker. There are two reasons for this. First, Movie Maker comes free with every copy of Microsoft's Windows Millennium Edition (or Windows ME). Second, although it is limited compared with more expensive programs, Movie Maker is very good at compressing movies so that they can more easily be sent to friends as part of an email message or posted on an internet site.

WHERE CAN I GET MOVIE MAKER?

If you're using Windows ME, you don't have to do anything, because Movie Maker is already on the CD-ROM along with other accessory programs like WordPad and Paint. However, if you're using an earlier version of Windows, you won't have Movie Maker. If that's the case, consider upgrading to Windows ME or choosing another video editing program. (To get an idea see the box on alternative programs at the end of the book 🗋).

Other Video Editing Programs
69

INSIDE MOVIE MAKER

Movie Maker comes free with Windows ME and for that reason it's the program we're going to use throughout this book to capture, edit, and produce our home movie. So it's time to get better acquainted with Movie Maker's functions.

KEY FEATURES

❶ Button bar
In common with other Windows programs, Movie Maker uses buttons to make it easy to control its features.

❷ Save Movie
This button lets you choose whether you want to save your movie at high, medium, or low quality.

❸ Send
This allows you to include a movie with an email message or send it to a website. You'll need a modem and an internet connection to use these features.

❹ Record
Use this button to record footage from, for example, a digital camera that's plugged into your computer.

❺ Collections window
When you copy video (or sound) clips into Movie Maker they're automatically organized into "collections" (somewhat like the folders used elsewhere in Windows).

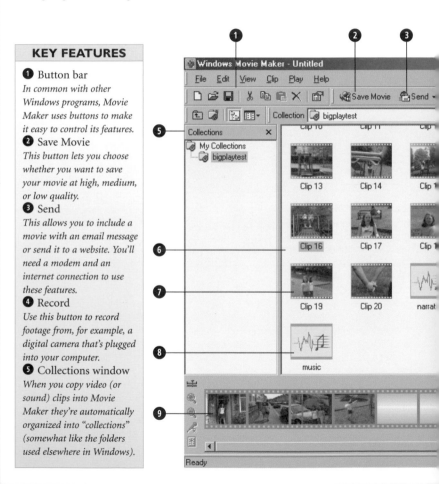

THE MAC ALTERNATIVE

Some iMacs ship with a wonderful video-capture-and-editing program called iMovie. It actually has a lot more features than Movie Maker (it has many more transitions, for example), and as a result it's capable of producing more sophisticated movies. On the down side though, iMovie can't match Movie Maker when it comes to producing ultrasmall finished movies.

Clip 16   00:00:00.00

KEY FEATURES

6 Inside a Collection
When a collection is highlighted in the Collections window (see 5) you can see the video and sound clips inside it.

7 Movie clip
This was copied from a digital camera and then stored in a collection. Movie Maker helps you identify each clip by showing the first frame.

8 Sound clip
You can add narration, background music, or sound effects to your movie.

9 The Storyboard
Designed to look like a strip of film, this is a visual representation of your home video.

10 Preview window
When you highlight one of the video clips in a collection, it's displayed here.

11 Preview controls
You can play, pause, stop, and rewind your video clip.

MOVIE MAKER'S PREVIEW WINDOW

Now let's look at two key components of Movie Maker's interface – the Preview window and the Timeline. As you work through this book, you'll become familiar with how both of them work very quickly; as we've said before, Movie Maker isn't exactly packed with features, but it's about the best there is for producing tiny home videos on a budget. We're going to cover the Preview window first.

KEY FEATURES

❶ The Preview window
Click on a clip inside a Collection and the first frame appears here. Double-click on the clip and it starts playing immediately.

❷ Current position
The pointer gives you a visual indication where you are in the clip that's being previewed. In the example shown here, we're about one-third of the way through the clip.

❸ Play
You click this button to start playing your clip.

❹ Pause
This button pauses play.

❺ Stop
And this button stops your clip.

❻ Back
This moves you to the beginning of the clip.

❼ Forward
This moves you to the end of the current clip.

Clip 16

UNDERSTANDING COLLECTIONS

Collections are a little like Windows shortcuts – when you look inside a collection at the video and sound clips, what you're seeing are pointers to the original captured from your DV camera, rather than the files themselves. When you delete video or sound clips from a collection, you're just deleting the pointers – the actual file remains stored in Windows' My Video folder. If you want to throw them out completely – perhaps to save space – open that folder and drag the files to the trash can.

KEY FEATURES

8 Previous frame
Clicking this button will take you back through your movie a frame at a time.

9 Next frame
Click this button and the clip will advance by a single frame. This feature is useful for finding specific frames in your movies, and it allows you to perform extremely precise edits.

10 Full screen
This feature allows you to play back video using the entire screen.

11 Split clip
To divide a clip into two or more parts, use the Play controls to move to the right point and then click the Split Clip button. It "cuts" the clip in two like a pair of electronic scissors.

12 Time
Here's the current position in the video expressed in hours, minutes, and seconds.

00:00:04.27

MOVIE MAKER'S TIMELINE

The Timeline is a key component of Windows Movie Maker. Basically it allows you to see your entire movie in miniature and allows you to make judgments affecting the overall narrative. Clips stored in the Collection window can be dragged and dropped onto the Timeline using the mouse. Once the clips are in position you can watch this "rough cut" of your film before making further fine adjustments.

KEY FEATURES

1 Timeline
The Timeline shows the length of your movie, expressed in hours, minutes, and seconds.

2 Toggle switch
This switch moves you between the Timeline and Storyboard view.

3 Zoom in
This button means you can work in more detail on just a few clips in the Timeline.

4 Zoom out
This button allows you to see more of the Timeline.

5 Record narration
Click on this button to open a dialog box, which lets you record new sounds using a microphone.

6 Set audio levels
This balances the sound between what was originally recorded with the video and what's been subsequently recorded as, for example, a narration.

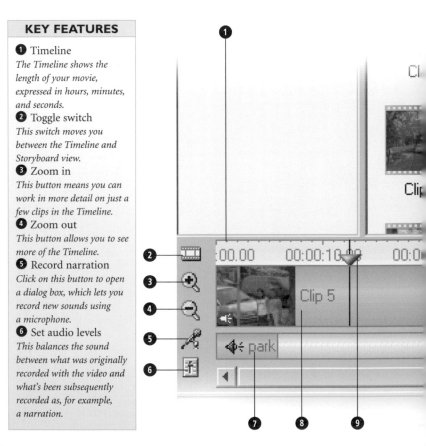

BACKING UP

As with all applications on the PC, if you want to delete the sound and video clips used by Movie Maker, you have to make a conscious effort to do so. However, you'll also be familiar with what can happen when a computer crashes – at worst you can lose everything you've been working on. For this reason, it's always wise to make periodic copies of your movies. Consider investing in a Zip drive, which is convenient and inexpensive.

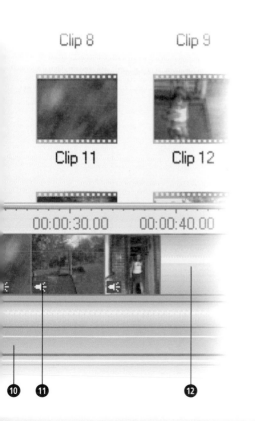

Clip 8   Clip 9

Clip 11   Clip 12

00:00:30.00   00:00:40.00

⑩   ⑪   ⑫

KEY FEATURES

❼ Narration
This section of the Timeline is reserved for sound that's been recorded using a microphone, usually a piece of narration.

❽ Long clip
Movie Maker uses the first frame of a clip to help you identify it. Longer clips are represented as a frame plus a gray rectangle, with the name of the clip as a label.

❾ Current position
This line indicates the current position the movie has reached as it plays back.

❿ Scroll bar
Drag this bar to the left or right with the mouse to navigate through long movies.

⓫ Speaker icon
This icon indicates that sound was recorded along with this video clip.

⓬ Empty slots
These are spaces in the Timeline ready to receive new video clips.

DV CAMERAS

A digital video camera is the best way to shoot home movies.
Picture quality is excellent and, because it records digitally, the
results can be copied to and then edited easily on a home PC.

GETTING ACQUAINTED

The video camera is the starting point for any home movie, whether you're capturing an event like a picnic or school concert or trying to devise and then film an original story. There are basically two kinds – analogue and digital.

From the outside, a DV camera is much like an old analogue camcorder. It has a zoom lens, and buttons for recording and playing back; it stores video on removable cassettes, can be equipped with extra attachments like a microphone or tripod, and can be connected to other devices like TVs, videos, and computers. Spend some time getting to know your camera. Your movies will benefit in the long run.

A modern DV camera with external microphone and LCD screen for previewing video footage.

However, there are important differences:

● Sharper pictures: a DV camera offers around twice the horizontal resolution of an analogue camcorder.

● Better sound: broadly speaking, it's like comparing an audio cassette and an audio CD.

● More accurate recording: a DV camera uses a special chip called a charge coupled device (CCD) to record what the lens "sees" and then stores it on tape as a series of 1s and 0s (a little like your computer when it stores anything on its hard disk). This results in a much more accurate recording.

● No degradation: because everything's stored digitally, it will look the same no matter how many times you watch it or how many times you copy it.

● Same format: it is digital, like a computer, so there's no conversion process when you copy from the camera to the computer. Thus, the version on the computer will be as good as the original was when you first recorded it.

● Still photographs: many modern DV cameras can take high resolution single photographs – they double as digital still cameras.

OPTICAL AND DIGITAL ZOOMS

Most digital video cameras have two kinds of zoom – optical and digital. Of the two, optical is the most useful. It works somewhat like a telescope – you have two lenses and one is moved relative to the other to zoom in and out of your chosen subject. The digital zoom takes over after you've reached the limits of the optical zoom and simply magnifies what you're already seeing. Thus, the more you zoom in digitally, the more you'll lose sharpness and definition. It has its uses, but a good optical zoom is more important.

A charge coupled device (CCD) chip

DV-IN AND DV-OUT

All DV cameras will have a DV-out connector that lets you plug them into a computer equipped with a 1394 controller (sometimes called an iLink or FireWire connector, and discussed in Chapter Three ◻). This is how you're able to copy your movie from the camera to the computer. However, only the more expensive cameras incorporate a DV-in, which allows you to copy the movie back out to the camera so you can then plug it into a TV or make copies onto other equipment.

Specific Features

Modern DV cameras include a very wide range of features, and it's worth spending some time evaluating the different models on the market before deciding which one to buy. Most models will suffice for general-purpose use, but if you have more professional aspirations, the quality of the lens and the optical zoom are key features to consider. Remember, too, that many DV cameras can also take still photographs. Your local camera store will be able to advise you on which model to buy.

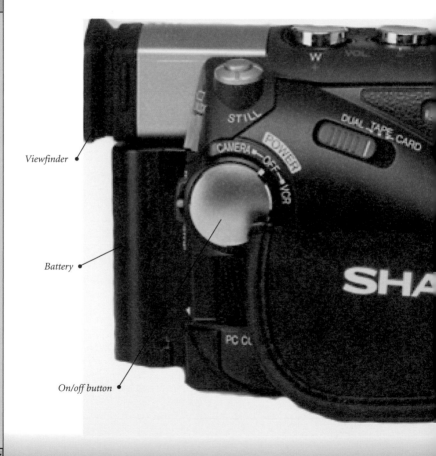

Viewfinder

Battery

On/off button

USING A WEBCAM

These days, many computers ship with a webcam – a small camera that's attached to the computer and can record video sequences right onto the hard disk. It has far fewer features than a normal digital video camera and most need to be hooked up to the computer permanently. However, if you already have a webcam on your computer and a copy of Windows ME (which includes Movie Maker), then you have everything you need to begin experimenting with digital movie making.

• The lens

• Wrist strap   Microphone •

DV cameras bring point-and-shoot video to everyone. Being able to edit your images with no loss of picture quality, as well as being able to add transitions, titles, narration, music, and special effects brings movie making right into the home.

CAPTURING VIDEO

Before editing your movie, you need to get the footage onto
your home computer. A digital video camera will plug right in
and copy your movie without any loss of quality.

PLUGGING IN

When it comes to connecting your camera
to your computer, there are a few simple
considerations to keep in mind. First, your
digital video camera will have the correct
connector, so you don't have to worry
about that. Your computer may also
include the necessary connector already,
but if it doesn't see the "My computer
doesn't have the right connector" box
on the following page.

DO YOU HAVE THE
RIGHT CONNECTION?

You can either check the
contents list that came with
your computer or start
Windows, then click on the
My Computer icon with
the right mouse button and
choose **Properties**. When
the **Properties** dialog box
opens, click the **Device
Manager** tab and you'll see
a list of devices (these are
the components in your
computer). Different
manufacturers call them by
different names but you
need to find an entry in the
list that's called something
like "1394 Controller" or
something similar.

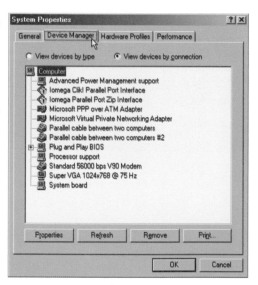

The other item you need is a cable, which is available from most computer stores. Just be aware that different computer manufacturers use different shaped connectors, so check your computer and your camera to make sure you buy the right one.

Finally, there's one other potentially confusing issue. The 1394 controller (that's the technical name for the element in the computer that you connect the camera to) can also be known by other names. For example, Apple calls it FireWire (and in fact the original 1394 specification was based on FireWire), while Sony calls it iLink. They're basically the same thing but may have different shaped connectors so, again, check them before you buy your cable.

Left, connecting the cable to the back of a PC.

Below, connecting the cable to the back of the camcorder.

The two ends of the cabling that link your camcorder to your PC.

MY COMPUTER DOESN'T HAVE THE RIGHT CONNECTOR

Some modern home computers include the necessary connector so that you can plug a digital video camera right in. If yours doesn't have this, then you'll have to buy a video capture card – a small circuit board that plugs into the main system board of your computer. If you don't want to take the lid off, get a more knowledgeable friend or neighbor to help out, or ask your local computer store to do it for you. The important thing is to get a card that is IEEE 1394-compliant, because this is the standard used for DV capture. The prices of cards start at under $100.

GETTING VIDEO INTO MOVIE MAKER

We've talked a little about how you can get digital video onto a home computer. Now it's time to transfer it with Windows Movie Maker. First, you need to shoot some home video, so we've included a few pointers in case you're stuck for ideas.

1 GETTING READY

● Go to the **Start** menu and load Movie Maker. Click on **Programs**, then **Accessories** to find it.

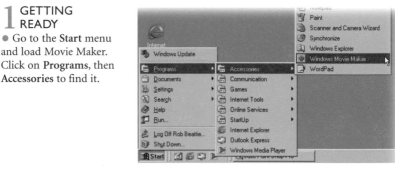

● Movie Maker loads up. It looks empty for now, but we'll fix that shortly.
● Plug in your digital video camera and switch it to play mode (it may also be called VCR mode). The first time you do this, there may be a pause and you may see your computer's hard disk light flashing. This is fine – it simply means that your computer and digital video camera are busy getting acquainted.

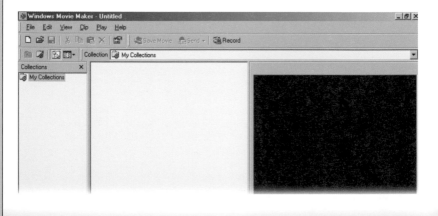

● Alternatively, you may see this screen. Depending on what you want to do, choose one of the three options. Because we want to go through the entire process, we're choosing **Do not record at this time**. Then click **OK**.

Windows Movie Maker ☒

A digital video camera or VCR has been detected. What would you like to do?

○ Automatically start recording my video from the beginning of my tape

○ Begin recording my video from the current position on my tape

◉ Do not record at this time

[OK]

● Click Movie Maker's **Record** button.

...vie Maker - Untitled

...iew Clip Play Help

...   📋 📋 ✕ 🔲 | 🎬 Save Movie 📧 Send ▾ | 🎞 Record

🔲▾ | Collection 🗐 My Collections

✕

● Again, Movie Maker asks you what you want to do. For now, choose the third option – **Use Default Recording Device**. Then click **OK**.

Windows Movie Maker ☒

A digital video camera or VCR has been detected. What would you like to do?

○ Automatically start recording my video from the beginning of my tape

○ Begin recording my video from the current position on my tape

◉ Use Default Recording Device

[OK]

STUCK FOR MOVIE IDEAS?

Many internet sites contain home videos that have been created using Movie Maker. A few minutes of grainy home video can be more inspirational than a Hollywood blockbuster because it has more in common with what you're trying to achieve. Go to **http://www.microsoft.com/windowsme/guide/moviemakerlarge.asp** for a list of places on the internet where you can watch short videos – and post your own.

2 CHOOSING THE SETTINGS

● This is the point at which you define your settings needed for recording digital video. Our Sharp digital video camera has automatically been detected. If your DV camera isn't detected for some reason, click the **Change Device** button.

Record [×]

Record: Video and audio ▼

Video device: Sharp DV Device
Audio device: Sharp DV Device

[Change Device...]

☑ Record time limit: 2:00:00 ⬍
☑ Create clips

☐ Disable preview while capturing.

Setting: Medium quality (recommended) ▼

Video for e-mail and dual-channel ISDN (128 Kbps)

320x240 pixels
15 frames per second

404 hrs 57 min available on drive C:

Elapsed 00:00:00   ● Record 📷

Digital video camera controls
▷ ❚❚ ■ ◁❚❚ ❚❚▷ ◁◁ ▷▷

Cancel

● When you click the downward pointing arrow, you'll see a list of available devices. Since we've only ever attached our Sharp DV camera to our computer, that's the only one listed. Select it by clicking on its name.

Change Device [×]

Video: Sharp DV Device ▼ [Configure...]
Sharp DV Device

Audio: ESS Allegro ▼

Line: Microphone ▼

OK

● Click the **OK** button to close the dialog box.

Line: Microphone ▼

OK

● Movie Maker usually records video at medium quality but it's best to try and use the highest setting your computer can handle. Click the downward pointing arrow.

● You can start by just selecting the recommended quality. However, here we're selecting **Other** to illustrate alternative settings.

● Click the drop-down menu to open the full list of settings.

● Choose the highest possible setting at the bottom of the list.

WHY MAKE A STORYBOARD?

A storyboard is essentially a series of drawings showing what is supposed to happen in each scene in your movie – rather like the illustrations in a comic book. Ideally, you should create a storyboard before you start shooting – even if it's just a written list of scenes it's better than nothing. It will help give your movie a better structure and start you thinking about camera angles and how best to set up scenes. You don't need to be any good at drawing in order to produce a decent storyboard because it's not the quality of the pictures themselves that is important. Rather, it gives you a chance to put your narrative ideas in some kind of order and lets you organize your long shots, close-ups, and so on. Storyboarding a home video in this way will undoubtedly save you time in the long run.

WHY THE HIGHEST SETTING?

Even though we're using Movie Maker to produce home videos that are small in size, the more information the program has to work with in the first place, the better looking the final product will be. So, if you have a modern, fast computer, you'll almost certainly choose the highest quality possible.

3 TIME TO PLAY

Make sure your DV camera is plugged in, switched on, and set to play back. Now it's time to control your camera and then record from it using Windows Movie Maker.

● Click the **Rewind** button to rewind the tape back to the start.

The Rewind button ●

● At this point you need to click the **Play** button. You'll hear the digital video camera start to roll. It shouldn't be more than a moment or two before the video you've shot starts playing in the **Preview** window.

● You can use the **Digital video camera controls** to pause, rewind, and fast forward your camera. You can even move back and forth one frame at a time. Try clicking the **Pause** button.

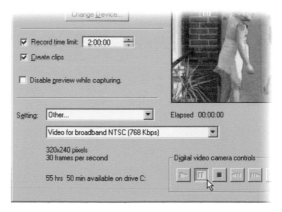

● When you've reached the end of the video that you want to record, click the **Stop** button.

● The **Save** dialog box opens on-screen.

● Type in a name for your captured video into the **File name** box. (We've decided to call ours "Playground" because it's about two girls playing in a park).
● Click the **Save** button to close the dialog box and to save your video to your computer's hard disk.

READY FOR ACTION

Now it's time for Movie Maker to perform its magic. It's going to analyze the video footage you've copied across to it and break the single chunk of video down into manageable scenes (called clips) so that your final movie is easier to edit.

● You'll see this dialog box as Movie Maker converts the footage into clips.

● When Movie Maker has finished, the dialog box and progress bar disappear and you're left with a selection of clips in the main window. You'll notice that the last clip is highlighted and also appears in the Preview window.

● It's best to check each of the clips to make sure there aren't any unwanted glitches in the footage. You can use the scroll bar to move back to the first clip.

The scroll bar

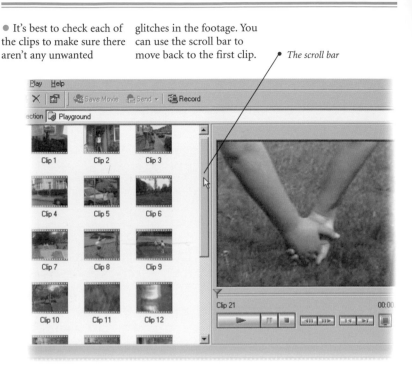

WHAT TO DO IF YOUR VIDEO QUALITY IS POOR

Once you've imported some video from your camera, play it back in the **Preview** window. If the video is jerky and the sound stutters, it may be that your computer simply isn't powerful enough to run Movie Maker properly. Don't despair – there are a few things you can try. First, make sure there are no other programs running at the same time as you're capturing video. Second, turn off the **Preview while capturing** option in the **Record** dialog box. Third, make sure you're capturing your video at the highest quality possible. Though this sounds odd, because it increases the file size of your movie, it may actually improve matters. Basically, it means your computer won't have to work so hard to compress the video as it captures it. You can always compress it later when you save the finished movie.

● Then, audition the clips in turn. Here, we've selected the second clip.

● Now we're playing back the second clip.

DISABLING CLIP CREATION

Movie Maker tries to help out by "watching" your video as it's captured and tries to determine where one scene ends and another begins.

In theory, you'll end up with a collection of clips that all start and stop at the beginning and end of the action. But it doesn't always work. If it begins to get in

the way, turn it off from the **Record** dialog box and you'll get a single clip of the entire movie instead, which you can then split up yourself 🗋.

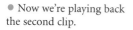

Trimming Clips

37

EDITING

Copying video from your camera to your home computer is just the beginning of the story. Now it's time to start turning the raw footage into a finished movie.

THE ROUGH CUT

You can cut your movie any way you like, but it's more fun to map it out roughly first by using Movie Maker's Storyboard feature. This is the section of the program that runs along the bottom of the screen and looks like a strip of film.

1 ADDING CLIPS

● Let's move **Clip 2** to the **Storyboard**. Click on it with the mouse.

● Click and hold the left mouse button down and start to drag **Clip 2** down to the **Storyboard**. As the cursor moves across the other clips inside the collection, you'll notice that it's turned into a circle with a line through it. This indicates that if you release the mouse button, the clip will simply stay where it is.

The cursor turns into a circle with a line through it

● Now the cursor is hovering over the first frame in the **Storyboard**; it has changed to an arrow with an open square and "+" sign next to it. This means that you can drop the clip here.

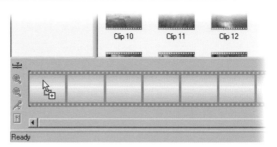

● Release the mouse button and move the cursor out of the way. Now you'll see a miniature representation of **Clip 2** sitting in the first slot of the **Storyboard**.

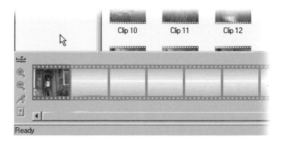

● Continue adding clips (in any order you like) until you have four or five positioned on the **Storyboard** like this.

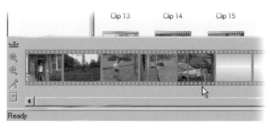

TRY A TRIPOD

Even those DV cameras that have built-in circuitry to cope with shaky hands will rarely deliver rock-steady video. Usually this won't matter, but for times when you need to show continuous smooth movement, for example, when following someone as they walk across a park or down the street, then it may be worth buying a tripod.

2 PLAYING THE ROUGH CUT

● Move the cursor to the first clip in the **Storyboard** and click on it with the right mouse button. From the pop-up menu, you then click on **Play Entire Storyboard/Timeline**.

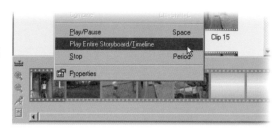

● Your rough cut will now play in sequence. You'll watch the actual clips in the **Preview** window and as the movie progresses, a yellow highlight moves from clip to clip on the **Storyboard**.

MAKING BETTER MOVIES

Good movies are rarely made in the editing room. Movie Maker is good at what it does, but even software as good as this cannot correct basic errors. To improve your results, get to know your video camera, and always shoot more scenes than you think you'll need. You'll be pleased that you did.

USEFUL SHORTCUT KEYS

As you get into Movie Maker, you'll discover that there are ways to get the program to do things without using the mouse. Here's a selection of useful keyboard shortcuts. To play or pause a clip press the [Spacebar]. To stop a clip completely, press the **period** key. To move to the beginning of a clip, hold down the [Ctrl] key and press the **Left arrow** [←]; to move to the end, use the [Ctrl] key with the **Right** arrow [→]. Move forward or back a frame at a time by substituting the [Alt] key for the [Ctrl] key. To play the video back full screen, hold down the [Alt] key and press the [Enter↵] key.

3 STORYBOARD REORDERING

● If the clips sitting in the **Storyboard** aren't in the right order, you can simply move them around using the mouse.

● We want to take **Clip 1** and move it so that it plays just before the last clip. Click on it with the left mouse button.

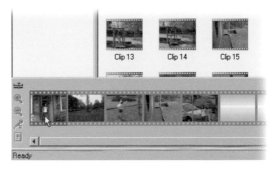

● Still holding the mouse button down, drag the clip along the **Storyboard**. An open rectangle appears next to the cursor (indicating that we're moving something), and a vertical blue line has appeared between **Clips 2** and **3**.

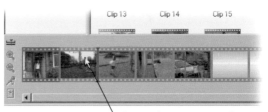

● *A rectangle appears next to the cursor*

● If we let go now, **Clip 1** will be positioned between **Clips 2** and **3** – i.e., where the blue line is. Since we don't want to do that, continue dragging until the blue line is just in front of the last clip.

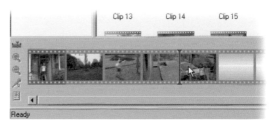

● Let go of the button and the clip drops into place.
● You can move clips around the **Storyboard** like this as much as you like.

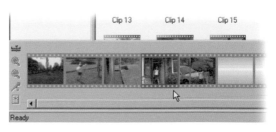

4 CLEARING THE STORYBOARD

To remove clips from the **Storyboard**, simply highlight them and then use your computer's Delete key. Remember – although you're deleting the clip from the **Storyboard** – it remains safely stored in the **Collection** 📄.

● Let's get rid of the first clip. Click on it with the left mouse button to select it.

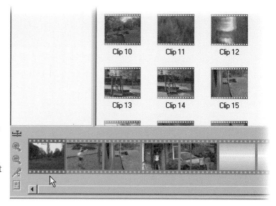

● Press the Delete key and the clip disappears.
● Now repeat the process until you've removed all the other clips.

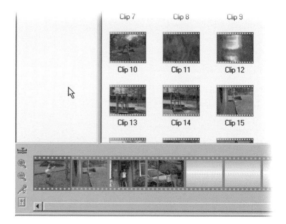

KEEPING MOVIE MAKER UP-TO-DATE

You'll get the best out of Movie Maker if you make sure it's an up-to-date version. Use Windows Update to keep your whole system current with the various upgrades, virus protection software, and feature updates that Microsoft provides for free. To load Windows Update, simply click the **Start** button and choose it from the pop-up menu. Naturally, you'll need access to the internet to use this feature.

41 **Understanding What's Stored Where**

THE FINAL CUT

Now it's time to get really organized. In this section we're going to give our video clips more meaningful names, trim the length of those clips that are too long, and arrange them in a final order to create a compelling movie. For the final touch, we'll include a transition to make one scene fade into another.

1 RENAMING YOUR CLIPS

● The more organized you are, the easier it's going to be to get your movie into shape. Start by giving your video clips names that make sense.

● Click on **Clip 2** with the right mouse button.

● When the pop-up menu appears, choose **Rename** by clicking on it.

● You'll see a little box appear around the words **Clip 2**. Now, they're also highlighted in blue. This indicates that they're ready for editing.

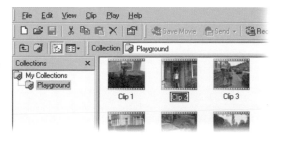

● Since the two girls in our clip are leaving the house, and it's the only time they do so in the entire movie, we're going to rename the clip as "Leaving." Simply type the new name in using the keyboard. All the clips can be renamed in the same way.

2 DELETING CLIPS

● Our first clip doesn't belong with the rest. That's because it is some film we shot somewhere else to make sure the camera and cassette were working. But it's of no use to us, so let's get rid of it. Click on **Clip 1** with the right mouse button and from the pop-up menu, select **Delete**.

● Movie Maker pops up a dialog box to ask if you're certain that you want to remove the clip from the **Collection**. We do, so click on the **Yes** button.

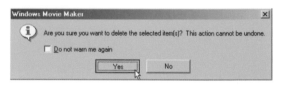

● **Clip 1** is removed from the **Collection** which now starts with the "Leaving" clip.

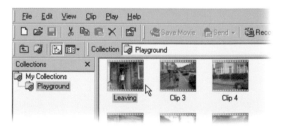

3 TRIMMING CLIPS

● It's unlikely that your video clips are exactly the right length, so it's useful to be able to trim them and remove unwanted footage at the beginning or end of the clips. You may also find that you have some extraneous noise at the beginning or end – perhaps where you shouted "Action!" This section shows you how to trim the beginning of a video clip so that it starts a few seconds later.

● First, play through all of the clips in the **Collection**. If there are any that are unwanted, delete them as described on the previous page. Then rename all of the remaining clips in the **Collection**, which we covered earlier ⬚. Now, when we played the clips back we noticed that there was some unnecessary noise at the start of the **Flowers** clip. Here we've selected it by clicking on it.

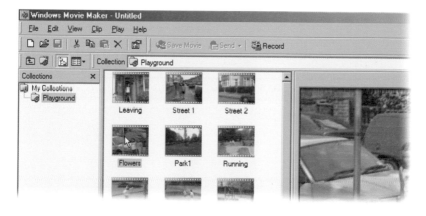

CREATING A TITLE

Every movie needs a title and you can make one using Paint, which comes free with Windows ME. To load Paint, click on the **Start** button, choose **Programs**, then **Accessories**, and click on **Paint**, which is on the subsequent menu, to load it. It's not the most sophisticated way of doing it, but you can create a colored background and then type in text on top of it easily enough. If you're unsure of how to go about it, click on Paint's **Help** button for more information on changing colors and adding text. When you want to import the title page into Movie Maker, please refer to Adding Music to Your Movie in the next chapter ⬚. The procedure for importing a title into Movie Maker works in the same way – the only difference is that you'll retrieve the title from your **My Pictures** folder.

---

35 Renaming your Clips

52 Adding Music to your Movie

● Click the **Play** button, which sits underneath the **Preview** window to play the clip back.

● Click the **Pause** button at the point you want to trim the clip.

● You'll almost certainly need to make some fine adjustments. Use the **Next Frame** button to move forward a frame at a time. If you need to go back, use the **Previous Frame** button.

● When you've gotten to the right spot, click the **Split Clip** button.

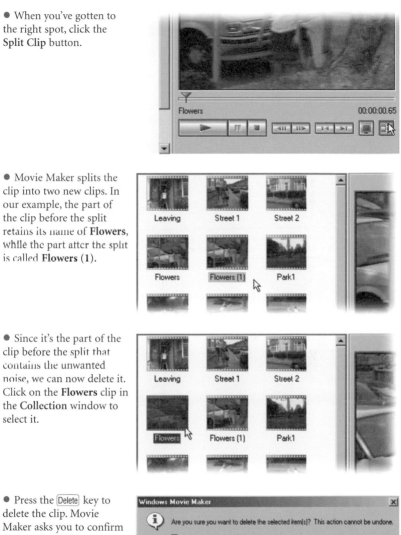

● Movie Maker splits the clip into two new clips. In our example, the part of the clip before the split retains its name of **Flowers**, while the part after the split is called **Flowers (1)**.

● Since it's the part of the clip before the split that contains the unwanted noise, we can now delete it. Click on the **Flowers** clip in the **Collection** window to select it.

● Press the Delete key to delete the clip. Movie Maker asks you to confirm that you really want to delete the clip. Click the **Yes** button.

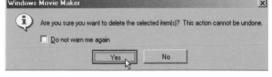

4 APPLYING TRANSITIONS

● Go through the rest of your video clips, checking their length and trimming them as necessary, as described in the previous section. Then, drag them in the correct order down to the **Storyboard**, which we covered at the start of this chapter ⌐|.

● Now we want to move from the **Storyboard** to the **Timeline,** which allows us to edit the clips at the bottom of the screen. Click the button that looks like a tiny ruler with a red triangle above it.

This button switches us to Timeline view

● This switches us into Movie Maker's **Timeline** view. You can see that while the clips at the bottom are still visible, they look different. For example, you can now see the relative lengths of the clips and there's a speaker icon to tell you when sound was recorded along with a clip. You can also see how long the overall video is by checking the measurements along the top (they're expressed in hours, minutes, and seconds). You'll also notice that the four buttons below the **Timeline** button are now active. We'll see how the two magnifying glass buttons work next. We'll move onto the others in the next chapter .

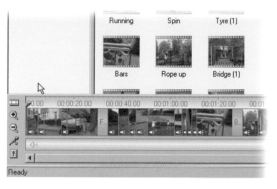

UNDERSTANDING WHAT'S STORED WHERE

It's a little complicated, but unless you've specified otherwise, it goes like this. Video that has been captured from your DV camera is stored in the **My Videos** folder. Movie Maker uses this footage to create clips that are stored in **Collections**. Collections are used to create finished Movie Maker projects, which are also stored in the **My Videos** folder. Deleting a project or a clip or a collection does not affect the original captured video. That stays safe.

● We want to create a special effect (known as a transition) that fades the second clip (ours is called **Street 1**) into the third clip (called **Street 2**). In order to do this, we need to zoom in on the clips so we can see them more clearly. Click the **Zoom** button.

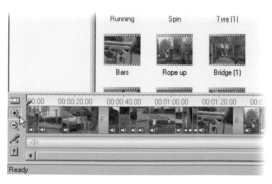

Recording a Narration

● We can now see the two clips more clearly.

● It's still not enough though, so click the **Zoom** button again, and when the clips have been enlarged, select the third clip (ours is called **Street 2**) by clicking on it.

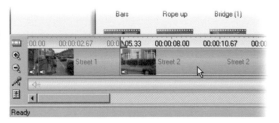

● In order to create a fade between the two clips we literally drag the second one to the left so that it overlaps the clip before it. Click and hold the left mouse button down and drag the clip slowly to the left. You can see that the degree of fade is expressed by a diagonal line.

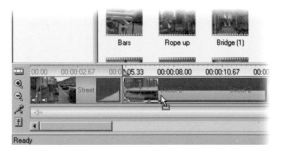

● When you think the overlap is about right, let go of the mouse button. You'll now see that part of the clip has a faded look – this indicates how much of the clip will be faded in on top of the previous clip.

● Click the **Timeline** button to move back to the **Storyboard** view.

● Place the mouse cursor over the first clip and click with the right mouse button. Choose **Play Entire Storyboard/Timeline** from the pop-up menu.

● Look in the **Preview** window and you'll be able to see where the two clips overlap, producing an effective transitional fade.

5 SAVING YOUR MOVIE

● Finally, to save the movie click on the **Save** button.
● Movie Maker opens its **Save Project** dialog box and saves your video as a **Project**. In this way, you can arrange the clips in your various **Collections** in different ways and save them as **Projects**.
● Naming it for our movie stars, we'll call it "Marion and Rose." Then we click the **Save** button.

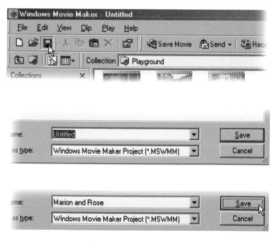

ADDING SOUND

Although you've already recorded sound along with your home movie, you'll almost certainly want to add some more. This chapter explains how to include narration and music.

RECORDING A NARRATION

Most home computers will include an external microphone (or if you're using a laptop computer, it will probably have a built-in microphone of some kind).

Movie Maker allows you to record different sounds and then save them with the video clips in your collection so that they can be incorporated into the film.

1 PREPARING TO RECORD

● Connect your mike to the "mic in" socket on your sound card. If you have problems, see the "When You Can't Record Anything" box 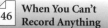.

● Load Movie Maker and choose **Open Project** from the **File** menu. Select your **Project** from the list by clicking on it and then click the **Open** button.

● Now click the **Timeline** button.

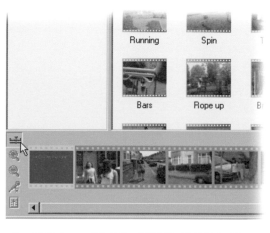

● This button activates the **Record Narration** button at the side. Now you need to click on that.

● This dialog box appears. Make sure that the **Line** input has the word **Microphone** next to it. If it doesn't, you'll need to follow the steps in the "How to record with your microphone" box below. Speak into your mike and watch the level indicator – the louder you speak, the higher it goes. For a good level, keep the volume at around halfway up in the green zone.

Record Narration Track

Device: ESS Allegro
Line: Microphone

Change...

109 hrs 05 min available on drive C:
Elapsed 00:00:00
☐ Mute video soundtrack

Record level

● Record   Cancel

2 MAKING A RECORDING

● This couldn't be easier. Just make sure you know what you're going to say, then press the **Record** button and start speaking. For simplicity's sake, we're only going to speak over the opening sequence of our movie, though you can, of course, prepare and record a narration for the entire film.

Record Narration Track

Device: ESS Allegro
Line: Microphone

Change...

109 hrs 05 min available on drive C:
Elapsed 00:00:00
☐ Mute video soundtrack

Record level

● Record   Cancel

HOW TO RECORD WITH YOUR MICROPHONE

If you can't record using the microphone, then when the **Record Narration Track** dialog box appears, click the **Change** button. When the next dialog box opens, find the **Input Line** section and click the downward pointing arrow. This will open up a list. Select **Microphone** from the list by clicking on it. Then click **OK** to confirm your changes.

● As you speak, you'll see
the movie playing back in
the **Preview** window and
the current position marker
moving along the **Timeline**.
Since we only want to
record over the opening
sequence, we've clicked
Stop when the current
position marker has nearly
reached the end of that clip.

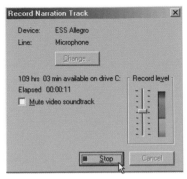

● When you click the **Stop**
button, the **Save Narration**
window opens.
● Type in the name for
what you've recorded
(we've simply called ours
Narration) and then click
the **Save** button.

WHEN YOU CAN'T RECORD ANYTHING

Windows may need to be
told that you want to
record something using a
microphone. To do this,
find the speaker icon in
Windows' **System Tray** at
the right-hand end of the
Taskbar and double-click

it. Choose **Properties** from
the **Options** menu, and in
the box that opens, click in
the empty circle next to
Recording. Click **OK** to
close the box. When the
Recording Control dialog
box appears, make sure the

Microphone has been
selected as the preferred
recording device. If it
hasn't, click on the empty
box next to **Select** so a
tick appears. Then click
the little "x" at the top
right to close the box.

3 USING YOUR RECORDING

● The **Narration** is saved
and appears in the central
Collection window along
with your video clips. Click
on it with the mouse.

● Since we want the
narration to start at the
beginning of the film,
we hold down the mouse
button and drag the
sound clip down onto the
"channel" next to the
microphone icon and
underneath the Timeline.

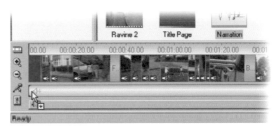

● Let go of the mouse
button and the sound clip
automatically drops into
the correct position.

● Right-click on the first
clip and select **Play Entire
Storyboard/Timeline** from
the pop-up menu.

● As the video plays back, you'll hear your newly recorded narration as well.

FINDING EXTRA SOUNDS

The internet is a really great source for high quality sounds that can be used, royalty-free, for personal projects. Look for good background sounds that may be difficult to record live – like waves crashing against the shore, or the wind in the trees. For a more dramatic – or even comic – effect you can go for high impact sounds like gunshots, car crashes, horses hooves, a scream, or footsteps. And there's nothing wrong with adding a little extra applause to a school concert from time to time. Take a look at **www.acoustica.com/ sounds.htm** or visit **http://users2.ev1.net/ ~prank/freesoundeffects. htm** – both of these sites offer a varied selection. Alternatively go to **www.soundfx.com/ freesoundfx.htm** which allows you to search for specific sounds from the home page.

MICROPHONE QUALITY

The built-in mikes used by modern DV cameras are excellent, especially at picking up ambient sounds like birds singing or crickets chirping. However, they can be less effective if what you really want is to hear what someone is actually saying against that background noise. It may be time to invest in an external microphone. Most cameras have a socket for one. However, it's not a bad idea to think of getting a good microphone for your computer anyway, especially if you plan to record lots of narration.

ADDING MUSIC FROM A CD

You can enhance the quality and the atmosphere of your movie with some good background music. Windows makes it easy for you to record a track from a favorite CD that can be saved and then incorporated into your film.

1 PREPARING TO RECORD

● Get a music CD and put it in your computer's CD-ROM or DVD-ROM drive. What usually happens is that Windows recognizes you've loaded a music CD and assumes you want to start listening to it. A program called Media Player loads automatically and starts playing the CD at track one. If the program doesn't load, then follow the steps in the "Media Player didn't load" box ⌐.

● Here's Media Player playing the first track of our music CD.

● Click the **Stop** button and then click on the **CD Audio** button on the left of the screen.

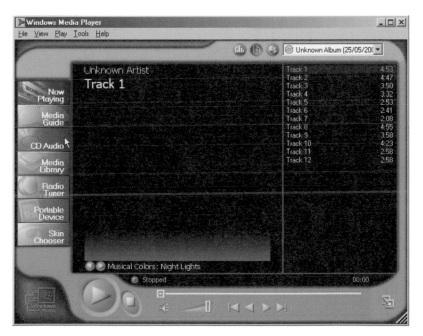

• Media Player lists the tracks on the CD in the middle of the screen. It puts a check mark beside each track in case you're ready to copy them all across to your computer's hard disk. In this case we only want to record one track, so let's get rid of the check marks by clicking on them, starting at Track 1.

• Continue removing the check marks until there's only one track left. We've chosen Track 6 because it sounds nice and is almost the same length as our movie.

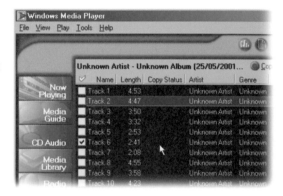

MEDIA PLAYER DIDN'T LOAD

Depending on how your copy of Windows is set up, Media Player may not start automatically when you load a music CD in your computer's CD-ROM drive. This doesn't mean there's anything wrong, it's simply one of Windows ME's many options that hasn't been switched on.

It's easy to get around this – just load Media Player manually by going to the **Start** menu and then choosing **Programs**. When the submenu opens, you'll see **Media Player** in the list of programs there. Click on the name and Media Player loads immediately.

COPYRIGHT

Although the law is different in each country, bear in mind that if you're recording a soundtrack directly from a music CD that you bought, you should respect the copyright of the author and publisher and act in accordance with the copyright laws.

2 RECORDING A MUSIC TRACK

● Click the **Copy Music**
button to start making a
digital copy of Track 6 on
your computer's hard disk.

● Media Player indicates
how much of the track has
been copied.

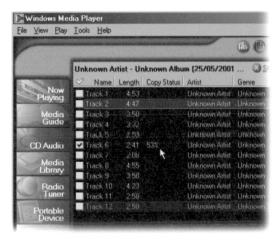

● When it's finished, Media
Player displays a message –
Copied to Library.
● You can now close Media
Player by choosing **Exit**
from the **File** menu.

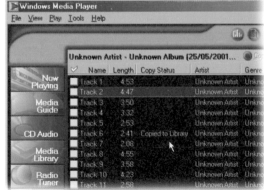

PREPARING TO RECORD FROM A CD

Before you record music from a CD, you need to make sure that one of Media Player's options is switched off. With the program loaded, go to the **Tools** menu and select

Options. When the **Options** dialog box opens, click on the **CD Audio** tab at the top. Find the **Enable Personal Rights Management** option, and make sure there isn't a

check mark next to it. If there is, remove it by clicking on the check mark with the left mouse button. Then click on the **OK** button to close the dialog box.

3 ADDING MUSIC TO YOUR MOVIE
● Switch back to Movie Maker and choose **Import** from the **File** menu.

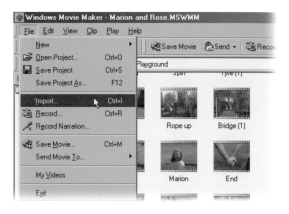

● Windows opens this dialog box. Media Player stores the music it copies several folders deep inside the **My Music** folder. Open that folder by double-clicking on it with the left mouse button.

● In our example, the **My Music** folder contains one called **Unknown Artist**. Double-click on that to open it.

● Inside that is another folder called **Unknown Album**. Double-click on that to open it.

● Here's the track we recorded. Double-click on the track to import it into Movie Maker.

MAKE MUSIC TAKE UP LESS MEMORY

Music files are usually big and can dramatically increase the size of your movie overall. One simple trick to reduce the size is to use the same piece of music twice or even three times in a single movie. Since all Movie Maker does is insert a "pointer" to the sound every time it occurs in your video, you only need to store it once – no matter how many times you decide to use it.

4 EDITING SOUNDS

● We want to add the music after the narration at the beginning of our movie, but there's a problem. We accidentally left the recorder running for a few moments after we'd finished speaking, so our narrated soundtrack is a little too long. Before we can slot the music track in next to it, we need to trim it slightly.

● We double-click on the **Narration** sound clip in the **Collection** window to start it playing.

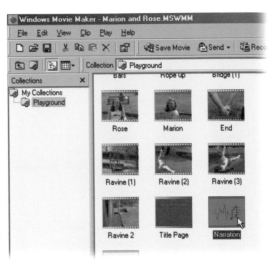

● When we get to the moment where we actually finish speaking, we click the **Pause** button.

● Next, click the **Split Clip** button to divide the sound into two clips.

● Movie Maker splits the sound into **Narration** and **Narration (1)**. Click on the second one with the mouse button to highlight it. Then press [Delete].

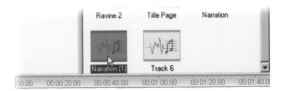

● Movie Maker asks if you're sure you want to delete the clip. Click the **Yes** button.

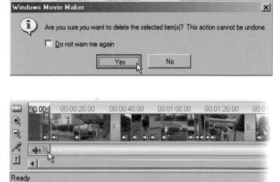

● Now we need to remove the original sound from the **Timeline**. Click on it with the left mouse button to highlight it. Then press Delete.

● Next, click on the **Narration** clip (remember, this is now the new, shorter version of the narration) and drag it down to the beginning of the **Timeline**.

● Release the mouse and the new, shortened narration slots into place.

5 FINISHING YOUR SOUNDS

● Now let's rename our music clip. Click on it with the right mouse button and choose **Rename** from the pop-up menu.

● Movie Maker high-lights the name of the sound and you can simply type a new name over it. We've chosen **Music.**

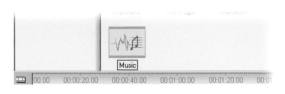

● Click on the **Music** clip and then, still holding down the left mouse button, drag it down to the **Timeline**, after the **Narration** sound clip.

● The sound clip slots into place and is ready to play alongside the video. Click on the first frame with the right mouse button and choose **Play Entire Storyboard/Timeline** from the pop-up menu.

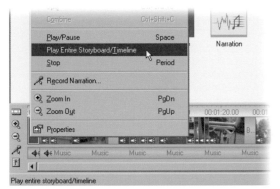

● The video then plays along with the narration and the music.

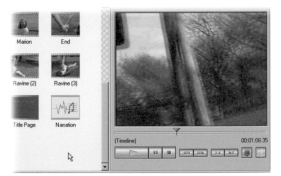

● Unfortunately, the music lasts slightly longer than our movie, so we need to cut it. Click on the music soundtrack to select it.

● Next, click on the gray triangle at the top of the **Timeline**. This indicates where the music currently finishes. Click on it with the cursor and you'll see it change to a double-headed arrow.

The gray triangle changes to a double arrow •

● Make sure you're still holding down the mouse button and then drag to the left. You'll see the triangle changes color from gray to blue. As you drag it to the left, you'll see the length of the music soundtrack decrease.

The triangle changes from gray to blue •

● When the triangle's lined up with the end of the final clip, let go of the mouse button. The music will now end when the movie does.

WHAT KINDS OF SOUND FILES CAN I USE?

You can use all the well-known ones, including Windows WAV files, those created using Media Player, and those stored in the superpopular MP3 format. You can recognize these files because their names will have the relevant extensions – for example SOUND.WAV or SOUND.MP3.

WATCHING YOUR MOVIE

This chapter explains how you can watch your movie on your own computer, send it to friends as part of an electronic mail message, or copy it to a website where anyone can watch it.

FLEXIBLE FILMS

Unlike conventional home movies, which you can only watch on television, films created and edited using digital technology can be enjoyed anywhere there's a computer. All modern computers are powerful enough to play back movies, and if you have an internet account, you can easily share them with your friends.

1 WATCHING IT AT HOME

Now it's time to save your movie so that anyone can watch it on a computer.
● Load Movie Maker and your movie project as described in Chapter 5 ⬏. Then click on the **Save Movie** button at the top of the screen.

● The **Save Movie** dialog box appears. For our purposes, we can leave all the settings as they are.

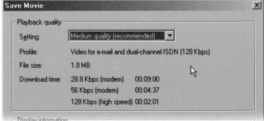

● You should give your movie a title though, so click in the empty space to the right of **Title** in the **Display Information** part of the box and type one in. We've called ours **A Day In The Park**.

Save Movie

Playback quality

Setting: Medium quality (recommended)

Profile: Video for e-mail and dual-channel ISDN (128 Kbps)

File size: 1.8 MB

Download time: 28.8 Kbps (modem) 00:09:00

56 Kbps (modem) 00:04:37

128 Kbps (high speed) 00:02:01

Display information

Title: A Day In The Park

Author: Rob Beattie

Date: 05/30/2001   Rating:

Description:

● Then click the **OK** button to carry on and start saving your movie.

Author: Rob Beattie

Date: 05/30/2001   Rating:

Description:

OK   Cancel

● Next, you have to save the movie with a file name (this is different from the title name that you created earlier).
● Click in the **File name** section of the box and give your movie a name. We've called ours **Park**. Then click the **Save** button.

Save As

Save in: My Videos

History

Desktop

My Documents

My Computer

My Network Pl...

Playground

Windows Movie Maker Sample File

File name: Park

Save as type: Windows Media Video Files (*.WMV)

● Movie Maker begins to create your movie. It may take a little time – Movie Maker lets you know the progress it's making by displaying this progress bar.

● When it's finished saving the movie, it asks you if you'd like to watch it immediately. If you do, click the **Yes** button.

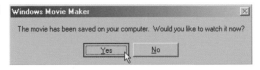

● Windows Media Player loads and starts playing your movie back. Notice that, although the file name for our movie is **Park**, the title that we chose (**A Day In The Park**) is displayed next to the movie window.
● When it's finished, or at any time, you can close Media Player.

IMPROVING PLAYBACK

Although you can't improve the quality of your video much after Movie Maker's finished with it, Media Player has some playback controls that you may find useful. With the video playing in Media Player, go to the **View** menu and choose the **Now** **Playing** tool, and select **Video Settings**. You can then experiment with the controls at the bottom of the window.

2 SENDING IT TO FRIENDS

So, you can play your movie back on your own computer, but Movie Maker also makes it easy to attach it to an email message that you can send to your friends.

● Go back to Movie Maker and this time, click the **Send** button at the top of the screen and then choose **E-mail** from the menu.

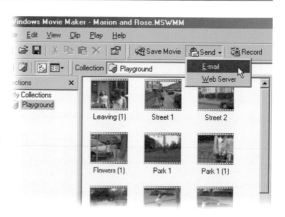

● When the **Send Movie** dialog box appears, you'll notice that it's the same as the **Save Movie** dialog box that we saw in the previous section. Again, give your movie a name (ours is called **A Day In The Park**) and then click the **OK** button.

● Movie Maker opens another dialog box and asks you to give the movie a file name. We've chosen **Park**. Then click the **OK** button.

● Movie Maker creates the finished movie.

● Here's the clever part. Movie Maker loads a dialog box listing all the electronic mail programs you're likely to have installed on your computer. We've chosen Outlook Express because it's the one that comes free with Windows ME. Just click on the name of your email program to highlight it and then click the **OK** button.

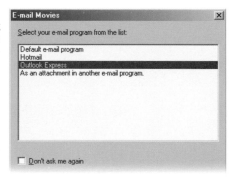

● Outlook Express opens a new, unaddressed email message with the movie already attached (you can see it listed in the **Attach** line as **Park.wmv**) and an explanatory message already in place.

● Click in the **To** section of the email message and type in the address of the person you want to send the movie to.

● Next, press the Tab key twice (you'll find it just above the CapsLock key on your computer's keyboard) and give your email a subject so that the recipient knows what it is.

● Then, click on the **Send** button.
● The message and attached movie are placed in the out box of your email program. The next time you load it to send and receive messages, they'll both be sent.

EMAIL ETIQUETTE

Friends with slow internet connections will not thank you if an extraordinarily large Movie Maker movie suddenly appears in their in box and takes an hour to download. If you must make your movies large ones, then it's only polite to send the recipient a text email message first to explain what you're going to do.

HOW LONG WILL A MOVIE TAKE TO EMAIL?

Movie Maker's pretty good at gauging how long it will take to send a movie attached to an email. If you look at either the **Save Movie** or the **Send Movie** dialog box, they gives an estimated delivery time. For example, our two and a half minute video is under one and a half megabytes in size and would take around four and half minutes to send to someone using a 56K modem. Keeping your movie files small will speed up the process.

3 POSTING IT TO THE INTERNET

Rather than sending the movie directly to friends and family, you can post it to a free internet site and then send them the address. That way they can watch the movie at their leisure.

● If you want to follow this section exactly, you'll need to create an account with POPcast, a service that lets you post your movies to the net for free. Please go straight to the "Creating a POPcast account" box ⬐.

● Go back to Movie Maker and click on the **Send** button. This time, choose **Web Server**.

● The **Send Movie to Web Server** dialog box appears. Essentially it's the same as the ones in the previous sections for **Save Movie** and **Send Movie**. Give your movie a title (ours is **A Day In The Park**) and then click the **OK** button.

Creating a
POPcast Account

● When the next dialog box appears, type in the file name of your movie (ours is called **Park**) and then click the **OK** button.

● Again, Movie Maker creates your movie, complete with narration and background music.

● This time, Movie Maker opens the **Send To Web** dialog box. This is a little more involved.

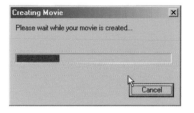

● Click the downward pointing arrow next to the **Host name** entry in the dialog box and choose **POPcast** from the list.
● If you haven't yet created an account with POPcast, refer to the "Creating a POPcast account" box over the page.

● Type your **User/login name** and **Password** in the dialog box and then click the **OK** button.

● Movie Maker dials your Internet Service Provider, makes the connection, and then starts to upload your movie onto the POPcast website.

CREATING A POPCAST ACCOUNT

It's actually very simple. You'll need a modem and an account with an ISP. Then, when the **Send To Web** dialog box appears, select **POPcast** as your host name and click the **Sign me up** button. This will take you to the POPcast website. You then have to fill in a simple form and come up with a **User name** and **Password** for your account – it's a good idea to write these down and keep them safe. After that you can switch back to Movie Maker and continue uploading your movie. At the time of writing, the POPcast service is free. You can explore the site at **www.popcast.com**.

• When the movie has finished uploading, you'll be taken automatically to the POPcast website. After a few moments – depending on the speed of your internet connection – your movie will load and then play.

• Click on the **My Account** heading at the top of the screen, and you'll be taken to a list of all your videos stored on the POPcast site.

● You can tell friends and family about your video by sending them an email message. Click the **V-MAIL** button and then fill in the form when it appears.

● Move between the fields using the [Tab⇄] key.

● Click on the **Send it in** button to send the message.

● When people open the message, they will see a link to your video. Clicking on it will take them directly to the POPcast site.

● You can also send your video to friends as part of an electronic greeting card.

● Click on the **V-GREET** button, choose a design and then follow the instructions to email the greeting.

● When you send a V-GREET message to a friend they receive an email telling them what you've sent and a link to the POPcast web site. When they click this link, their web browser is launched and they're taken straight to the website.

OTHER VIDEO EDITING PROGRAMS

Windows Movie Maker is good, but there are other programs that offer you much more sophisticated control over capturing and editing digital video. For example, they'll include a greater range of special transition effects, which help you to switch smoothly between scenes; some may even offer Hollywood-style features like fast and slow motion. There are many different products available, but those to consider include MGI's VideoWave, Pinnacle's DV Studio range of products, Ulead's Video Studio, and Adobe Premiere. For newcomers, some of these companies offer combination products that include the software, a video capture card, and a cable. Your local computer store will be happy to advise you on suitable programs.

GLOSSARY

1394 CONNECTOR
Variously called Firewire by Apple and iLink by Sony, and most commonly known as a DV connector, this is the standard connector for copying digital video between devices. If you want to copy video from a camera to a computer, they must both be equipped with one of these connectors.

ATTACHMENT
The most common way of emailing finished movies to friends is to compose a message as usual and then click the "Attach" button – this allows you to add your movie to a message, somewhat like sending a package along with a letter.

CCD
Charge Coupled Device. The electronic part of a digital video camera that "translates" the images that the lens sees into the digital data (i.e., 1s and 0s) that are actually stored on the camera's cassette tape.

CLIP
Any short item used in your movie, usually comprising a sound or a piece of video.

COLLECTIONS
Movie Maker organizes the video, sound, and graphics that go to make up a movie into "collections." They're like the folders used by Windows itself. You can use more than one collection in a movie.

DIGITAL VIDEO OR DV
Video that has been recorded digitally. It retains the same quality no matter how many times you watch it, or the number of times you copy it.

DV-IN AND DV-OUT
All modern digital video cameras have a DV-out connector (see 1394 connector), which lets you copy video from them to a computer. Not as many have a DV-in connector, which lets you copy your edited movie back to the camera.

FOOTAGE
Historical, Hollywood-style, terminology for exposed film. When you use your camera you are "shooting footage."

FRAME
All moving video is actually made up of a sequence of still photographs, called frames. Movie Maker allows you to move through a movie frame by frame so that you can edit with greater precision.

MEDIA PLAYER
A free program included with various versions of Windows that can play back digital music and video. This means you and your friends can watch and listen to your finished home movies on a computer.

MOVIE MAKER
A simple, easy-to-use video editing program that's included free with every copy of Windows Millennium Edition.

MP3 FILES
A way of storing music digitally that is close to CD-quality. However, music recorded this way takes up much less space, making it very useful for movie sound tracks.

PROJECT
When you've finished editing your movie, all the items in all of the related collections (video clips, sound clips, and graphics) are saved into a single project.

STORYBOARD
A part of the Movie Maker program where you can arrange your video clips in different sequences while trying to determine the best order for them.

THUMBNAIL
This is a miniature visual representation of something larger. For example, Movie Maker represents its video clips with little postage-stamp sized photos; the photo itself is a miniature of the first frame in the clip.

TRANSITIONS
Special effects that occur between scenes. For example, Movie Maker is able to fade one scene out as it fades the next one in.

TRIMMING
The procedure whereby you slice the beginning or end of a video clip in order to get rid of unwanted footage.

WAV FILES
The format used by Windows to store digital sounds. If you record something onto your computer, it will be saved as a WAV file.

INDEX

ACKNOWLEDGMENTS

PUBLISHER'S ACKNOWLEDGMENTS
Dorling Kindersley would like to thank the following:
Paul Mattock of APM, Brighton, for commissioned photography.
Sharp Electronics (UK) Ltd for the loan of the VLME 10 Digital Camcorder
shown on pages 7, 16, and 19, and the VLME 100 PRO on page 14.
POPcast.com

Screen shots of Microsoft® Movie Maker used
by permission from Microsoft Corporation
Microsoft® is a registered trademark of Microsoft Corporation.

Every effort has been made to trace the copyright holders.
The publisher apologizes for any unintentional omissions and would be pleased,
in such cases, to place an acknowledgment in future editions of this book.

All other images © Dorling Kindersley.
For further information see: www.dkimages.com